For Janet
thank you for your Devotion
to helping our world get
better. I wish I
had more

THE GEOMETRY OF SPLITTING SOULS

Time to get
to know you,
much love,
Ibu Robin
come see me in
Bali Sometime

Poems by

Robin Lim

D1569289

BLUE LIGHT PRESS ◆ 1ST WORLD PUBLISHING

1st WORLD
PUBLISHING

SAN FRANCISCO ◆ FAIRFIELD ◆ DELHI

iburobin @ bumi sehat bali.org

1ST WORLD LIBRARY
809 S. 2nd Street
Fairfield, IA 52556
www.1stworldpublishing.com

BLUE LIGHT PRESS
1563 45th Avenue
San Francisco, California, 94122

BOOK & COVER DESIGN
Melanie Gendron
www.melaniegendron.com

COVER ART
Zion Lee

AUTHOR PHOTO
Margo Berdeshevsky

According to the Hopi tradition, the First World: "Endless Space" contained the First People and was a pure and happy universe. It was destroyed by fire. The name of Blue Light Press comes from the final stanza of a poem by Diane Frank: "And when I touch you / do you see / the blue light / around my heart?"

FIRST EDITION

LCCN: 2011943597

ISBN 9781421886343

ACKNOWLEDGMENTS

"The Bone Drum" appeared in *Short Fuse the Global Anthology of New Fusion Poetry*, Rattaphallax Press, 2002. "Stoop Berries" and "Painting Carolyn's Bedroom in August" appeared in *The Dryland Fish*, 1st World Library, 2003. Some of the "Tsunami Notebook" poems appeared *Contemporary Review*. *100 Poets Against the War*, Salt Publishing, 2003, included the poem, "Good Morning Middle Age" and "Sept. 11, 2001—An Embryo's Perspective". "Painting Carolyn's Bedroom in August" appeared in *Bamboo Ridge #81*, Spring 2002. *This Enduring Gift 2010* included; "Ode to Dry Starlight," "What Will Never Dry" and "Where They Hung a Crucifix". *Adanna Journal 2011* included, "Janet's Son Has Died".

Many of these poems are featured in Deja Bernhardt's films: Guerrilla Midwife and Tsunami Notebook, www.skwattacamp.com.

The author wishes to thank many dear poets, artists and songwriters for their support, and for grace: Wil, Hemmerle, Margo Berdeshevsky, Theodore Sturgeon, John Briley, Marilyn Hacker, Elizabeth Gilbert, Michael Franti, Mangku Ketut Liyar, Joel Garnier, Devin Bramhall, Marjorie Evasco, Nguyen Bao Chan, Alvin Pang, Ed Maranan, Nori Nakagami, Ronald Baytan, Jan Francisco, Nancy Cook, Viktor Tichy, Thor Hemmerle, Lakota Moira, Gede Robi, Zhòu Lee, Noël Bernhardt, Wine Pramiyanti Bernhardt, Hanoman Hemmerle, Alfred Pasifico Ginting, Hannalore Josam, Liz Sinclair, Nancy Cummings, Chuck Miller, Alice Walker, Christine Wadsworth, Bruce Grady, Kadek Krishna Adidharma, Gary Whited, Katherine Bramhall, Nancy Cummings, Marie Zenack, , Cresencia Lim Jehle, Christine Jehle Kim, Déjà Bernhardt. Who says a good muse is hard to find?

Melanie Gendron, thanks for Book Design, Zion Lee for the cover, Diane Frank of Blue Light Press. . . thank you for believing in this patchwork of words. OM Saraswati & Mother Mary.

Contents

The Heartland, The Ring of Fire & All the Ripples From:

Dedicated to my baby sister,
Christine
—for whom I never could write a poem.

THE HEARTLAND,
THE RING OF FIRE
& ALL THE RIPPLES FROM:

Sept. 11, 2001—an Embryo's Perspective

A child hovers in the wine colored
wetlands of a belly.
His heart is working at 150 beats per minute.

In New York City
and in Washington, all the angels of our brief
history make a circle and bow their heads, crying.
My unborn grandson feels his mother's heart recede
from him. It is not a good time to be anyone.

My eyes are too dry, as if to cry
would be a selfish thing. After all, I am alive
and did not have to choose between fire, the weight of concrete
and steel, or raining from a high window.

My grandson sends me a tentacle,
as fine as a camel's eyelash but long and curling.
He reaches across time,
to tell me something in a language not of his mother's
people, and not any tongue his father speaks.

I bow my head along with the disappointed angels
and listen, and hope to make out his meaning.

STRETCH MARKS

My son paints me
on a canvas of wild black
hair and bone.
He chisels me from oil,
from a bit of red.

He lets one downcast eye
see him.

In thirteen years he's learned me.
How else could he paint sorrow,
tenderness, my harsh cheekbones, aging?
Kindly, he did not pencil in
the white hairs I've plucked,
the two divorces, lost twin babies
or a voice off key singing, "blackbird, blackbird."

ARMAGEDDON BALI . . . NINE MONTHS LATER

Wil comes home covered with something
I cannot see.
Even my famous nose cannot smell it,
but I know,
by the way he's aged
a century today,
by the sliding down corners of his eyes,
by how he boiled water for his bath
and scrubbed himself red,
that his work took him to Ground Zero
Indonesia.

Nine months after Bali shattered
like a painted egg,
I am busy receiving her babies.

The women come into labor late,
jittery, screaming more than ever I heard
at a thousand or more bloody birth doors.

Why do people create children
just when they know their world is ending?

Looking into the pregnant eyes,
I see the footage on their televisions;
images I did not watch before.
I see the remains of relatives and friends,
more than 200 dead and many more missing.
The glaze reflects the desperate search of husbands
seeking jobs, after hotels and restaurants
closed shop. Gardeners go home
to dream of rice fields long ago sold.
Unemployed waiters sell their sex cheaply,
to men seeking risky skin.

How else to pay the hospital,
which will not release the baby
until the bill is settled?

The boy born last night would not breathe.
I waited by his blue mouth until compelled
by what I think I know,
pushed in my own air and filled his lungs with kiss.
Today I must wonder, in a destabilized land,
what does it mean to breathe?
How can I do no harm now?

Learning to Master the Art of Exile

In the morning, before the smoke
of one hundred thousand
kitchen fires shrouds the island,
we can see Mount Agung.

Rusty truckloads of mandarin oranges,
snake skinned salak fruits,
mangoes, papayas, yellow meat melons,
red strawberries and purple manggis,
will come down from our mountain today.

These rich fruits will hit the market at sunrise
and start to rot immediately.
Some of them will come to my kitchen
carried by beggars seeking medicine.
My children and granddaughter will feast.

Sipping tea from a broken winged cricket cup,
I carry the weight of sin
of killing a mosquito—
the unbearable pressure of forgetting to be kind.

Nine months after the terrorist bombing,
Bali turns slowly, balanced on the back
of a female turtle
who calculates the geometry of souls splitting.
May all these babies
be born whole.

The Geometry of Splitting Souls

As a refugee
you have no genealogy left.
You will give your daughter any shelter you can
and sing to her half-remembered songs
in your mother's voice.

What kind of man, wanted in Timor,
dials a wrong number and finds a lonely girl
on the line?
What kind of man marries her in secret,
lays his head on the moon of her belly rising,
and steals a name for their baby?

Man, black as the Indonesian new moon sky,
you hate your boss and his money
but love yourself for working.
You can smile in seven languages
and cry in only one.

Woman heaved and crawled in circles
to bring the child Earth side
in a circle of pain and the midwife's desperate prayer:
    "We are only small people here. God,
    send your mother to help us before death comes
    to the screaming, breaking gate of amnion."

How will you treat this woman in five years time?
In seven?
Thirteen?
Her lips grown thin and her hands rough.

The soul is a single celled creature
with huge eyes.
Now go to the pay phone young man
and dial home.

WHERE THEY HUNG A CRUCIFIX

A daughter is valuable;
She can someday weave.

The sky is full of electric cables,
cement towers reinforced with steel.
The hairs on my arms rise
when I walk under such a night.
Sparks of lightning ricochet
between glass insulators crackling,
scolding, unzipping the sky.

This is the Indonesian power station slum
where the children of Sumba
live under leaking asbestos
like animals in stalls.
Here is the dirt floor
where women lean away
and weave blankets
dyed with dark roots,
on bamboo back strap looms.

Ibu Rika in labor, is unwinding all the indigo
threads of her life with Samuel,
and the harsh man before him.
Samuel picks lice from the head of
his smallest daughter.

Three walking children
go to school without rice.
There are no tourists
to buy their cloth.

Some of the men in the clan
come home with busted faces,
to watch television.

Christ was born in such a manger.
Christ was born in such a manger.

FOR WIL

I sleep with too many medicine herbs;
husband, you cannot see your place among them.

After many years, I feel myself
still falling into the amniotic fluid of you.

You swim away,
but damn it, I am the ripple on the surface
and the deep purple places.

You grow crimson wings,
lift yourself into the sky,
only to find the vast blue is our conjoined face,
streaked with jet streams.

I didn't notice it happening;
you became the window washer
of my heart's glass.

I feel myself going to seed—
about to drift away on a downy parachute.
You play guitar and penny whistle,

and wait for me on the rooftop.

GOOD MORNING MIDDLE AGE

I woke with a backache.
It's no use blaming the mattress,
I got older.
Here it is, the time I waited for, promising myself
that my peers and I would change the world.
From the clay of our hands and a few seeds of justice,
we would grow peace and food for the people.

Today I can't bear the pressure of listening
to my friends, my goddamned friends,
talking about meditation and art. Their heads twist
side to side, like puppets.
They do this because they woke up with backaches too.
They do this because they can't admit
that they really care about their two or three cars,
their DVD players, their vacation in Florida.

They earned their wealth, the right to ignore the lies.

The lie, that the United States elects a President,
and all the lies he tells, smiling on their TV sets.
The lie, that this nightmare will be over after the next election.
The lie, that demonizes an underfed Iraqi child,
who might, if we let her grow up, become a terrorist.
She might give birth to a whole litter
of terrorist pups, everyone of them with a grenade arm,
poised to take out your recreational vehicle with one thrust.

When Congress gives this so-called President
the infinite power to preemptively kill to protect our jobs
and our schools, where our children are taught
to talk about meditation and art,
these men will go home and try to have sex
with their wives, or someone, anyone.

Ignoring all the phone calls and the cries
of the constituents, our Senator
just wants to get it on. But this time,
having gone too far, having betrayed
every last dream, he can't get it up.

In the basement, his son, and all our American
babies, are huffing glue and household chemicals.

—December, 2000

FOR A BIRD CIRCLING THE SUN

When Margo became fifty-eight today,
a coin dropped into the inky
pool I keep way back inside.
The obsidian surface wrinkled
and rose up to birth a crone
wearing almost my face.

When I became thirty,
she gave me a card picturing
two old women at a cafe table—
checkered lives laid out for lunch.

We laugh at these two older women as
often as possible
over red wine, or darkly made tea.

We cannot laugh about the disgraceful
American wars our votes never
could stop. . .

but once, there were
dreams delivered by owls.

IN A DREAM OF GUATEMALA

Black Crow said,
"Come to the place where you were born.
Observe the color of your flesh emerging."

Is it oxygen rich pink? Gasping purple?
Cyanotic as a blue butterfly?

Were you pushed gently into the light,
or yanked with forceps,
cut out, pulled with suction?

Does your life tell a violent story?

How much have you learned to bow down?

One cannot count the particular shades of red.
From first to last breath, a crimson mosaic is built.

Were you ever given a rose?
Did you fall down on your new face?
Were you remembered in February
with paper hearts?

In the Mayan village of San Antonio Agas,
Doña Florentina's husband is dead from the war.
His body was found without hands.
After all the years, each time she hears a crow
Florentina looks for the hands in the roadside thistle.

Doña Viviana's husband is also dead from the war.
All the *conmadrones'*—the midwives' husbands
are dead from the war.

The widows' brick colored hands grind maise.
They eat tortillas with jackass bitters.
At births they burn copal,
pray to the Black Jesus
and wait for the "Rose of Jericho" to open.

Their hands make *huipils*;
leaning painfully away from the back strap looms
seated on palm mats, feet thrust forward in the dust,
their fingers choose red threads.

ANDREA'S FIRST MOON

Below the shadow of Mount Agua,
we're choosing ripe papayas,
roasted jackfruit seeds and knots of ginger root
at the Antigua market,
when Milvia comes crying,
"Andrea, only ten years old,
has bled."

We rejoice, "A new woman is among us."
Stupid Americans;
How can we know this mother
must hide her daughter's moon rags
from her drunken husband.

At four in the afternoon
on All Saint's Day,
a woman was raped 50 yards from their door.
Only men witnessed,
no one tried to stop it.
Is there a safe place for Andrea
to walk home from Santo Ignatius School?

We crones wipe the sweat
of our personal summers,
sip hibiscus water the color of lipstick,
and plan a Blessing-way.

We buy amber to burn,
a root of wild yam to offer,
an armload of golden *Ixtapul* flowers
and life everlasting.

Now candles, sold in seven sacred colors:
A blue one for the protecting angel;
Red to wish her love in the ripeness of time;
Green will bring her money;
Pink for the finer wishes;
White wax for her future children;
A yellow candle to burn for her health;
One black candle for each of her enemies.

Because Andrea is a woman,
we purchase many black candles.

First Full Moon Below the Equator

Reason says,
the moon can't be bigger
in Indonesia.

Yet, in the first days of pregnancy
with our boy,
the moon was huge,
a sonnet of light,
so large we worried
that the sun had gone nova.

Were the Americas roasting,
while we in Asia
saw only the reflection of too much heat?

We woke jittery,
made sweaty love, and walked
on narrow paths between
flooded rice fields.

Spread before us a checkered
mirror of mud was lit
by the pregnant moon
and fireflies mating.

When dawn arrived so normally,
you fed me one golden mango,
to celebrate the intact sun

and the whole world still living.

After ten years,
notice how our lovemaking
ripens clouds and
pulls hail from the sky.

THE BONE DRUM

The drum is killing me.
It calls me away without offering a destination.
The children are hungry
every few hours
and it's snowing again.

At the borders
we'll be asked to remove our shoes.
Our soles will be searched
for tattoos and plastic weapons.

During a brief time of peace
my ninety-six year old *Lola* spooned seven
heaps of sugar
into her coffee.
I raised an eyebrow.
She cocked her head toward the drumming
and said, "Better we gain some weight
while we can. We'll soon be fleeing."

Half breed refugees
hear distant pulsing in their placentas
driving blood into their fetus veins.
They kick their mothers
and make fists over seashell ears.

Born homesick,
I navigate without sextant
or stars.

APPLYING JOINT COMPOUND

If God wants a legal separation
I will divorce all of his beautiful faces.

First I'll turn my back on the blue-eyed face,
the one who poured warm sand over my flesh.
I'll leave behind the one planting rice
who plays handsome, flying fingers over guitar strings.
Faces pierced with bone and silver,
scraped smooth each morning, with razors,
one drop of holy blood, washed down the drain.

All the strong, sweaty and shirtless beings,
building temples, or out-houses,
can live without me.
They can hunt for their own food.

I'm busy filling the Yangtze, the Nile,
the Mississippi river with my birth water.

I dreamed that the only way to heaven
was to kiss.
Kiss wide and soft lipped.
Kiss with your nose, inhaling
the delicate scent of warm rice.
Don't expect to be able
to distinguish God from your lover.

When in pain from pressing against a bristly face,
put one drop of jasmine oil in your bath
and sing a ripple across the water.
It won't reach God's ear—remember the legal separation.
Women must talk to women, to birds and dolphins
and ordinary men.

The altar keeps moving.
We can never build it
except with snowflakes.

A Note to Sam Upon the Birth of His Son

I remember your eyes,
open like those of a nocturnal marsupial.
Like eyes I've glanced at by accident in the jungle
and never forgotten.
It was five or more years ago,
your wide eyes and trembling lips said, "Yes,
Ketut and I are lovers."

I saw your son then, in the eyes of my heart
seven pounds of God wearing dark hair
and mangosteen lips,
hovering purple, between birth and first breath.

I saw your wise fear
of the whole project.

I saw my hands, knots of ginger root,
receiving him into this world
of crumbling nations and bodhisattvas.
I suspect you saw him then too, sleeping in your DNA.

Upon his birth, my Ketut
split atoms with an eyelash.
Could you have predicted her bravery
by reading her star map?
A pity her day and time of birth, half a world away,
were never recorded in such a small Balinese village.
I remember how the road dust would cling to her legs as she walked
through the Monkey Forest in a pleated school skirt.
These days American dust craves her skin.

Sam, miracles of this magnitude
are serious business.

Your ancestors lit Sabbath candles,
kneaded course flour into bread,
both fat loaves and unleavened,
while hers planted rice and folded flowers into prayers.
All the *Zadies* and *Dadongs* lived entire lives,
to make way for this one boy.

All you can do now is inhale your son's scent,
and feel
the tears well up
and wash you.

PURPLE BALLOONS

"Sing again with your dear voice revealing a tone of some world far from ours, where music and moonlight and feelings are one."
—Percy Shelly 1822

First Tony died of AIDS, and then my cousin Junior.
In mourning, I made a pilgrimage
to the Gay Pride parade.

I saw posters preaching the gospel of masturbation,
men covered in only two sequin circles and a feather.
Bisexuals, cross dressers,
and then a 6 foot 5 inch beauty wearing 13 inch heels,
sporting hormone injection induced breasts
and a scar where her penis once grew.

There were women proclaiming their love for women
with roaring black motorcycles between their legs,
calling themselves "Dykes on Bikes."
I wanted to run up and give them helmets
and a warm cup of honeyed milk.
The crowd wanted to believe that a condom
would protect their hearts.

Two baby boys, each with a father and a daddy,
forced to suckle from bottles of infant formula.
I heard the big papa say, "We loved each other so much
we arranged to have a child—our child."
The others nodded their shaved heads
and commented on their commitments.

The Latino gays were by far the best dancers.
The Christian Fags Society sported metallic bull horns.
They thundered, "It's not your father's church anymore."

Men in chains and black leather pants
with no backsides, sold vibrators—toys in babe land.
I hope they wore sunscreen on their butts.

And then, the elderly parents of the Gay and Lesbian Family League
passed out stickers and free condoms,
bestowing support:
The sacrament of our times.
I wonder what all this has to do with the way two bodies curl
around each other when they sleep?

PAINTING CAROLYN'S BEDROOM IN AUGUST

Last Easter she called, confused, "Can't keep food down. Need help with a suppository. Can you come?"

I brought a small basket of hard-boiled eggs and one latex glove.

Until today, I've never admitted to myself that I resented being asked to insert that antiemetic suppository. I was feeling selfish, eating chocolate Easter rabbits with my children.

Carolyn had longed for a cherry red rag rug, which caught her eye in a little shop by the Des Moines River, in Bentensport. When the trees were bare in South-East Iowa, she would go there to count eagles. That day she saw fourteen predators.

When the headaches began, we went out for the medicine of pumpkin pie. She took hers without whipped cream—she was watching her weight. We blamed her illness on the disappointment she felt when someone else bought her rug. "Thou shall not covet thy neighbor's red rag rug." We laughed and boiled more water for tea.

I'm painting the ceiling apricot, it was her favorite color. In an apricot silk dress I saw her, before we were friends. She was a most beautiful woman. Her feet appeared pearl like, and she floated above the small white camellia appendages, as if she did not want to burden them.

The walls are the color her son calls "rice cakes." When I opened the can and looked into the round white, I recalled how she turned her bottom toward me, toward the medicine she needed, twisting gracefully, keeping her blue eyes on my face.

I did the dishes. Dried my hands. Started a load of laundry and called the neurologist. "I don't care if the MRI was normal." Knowing the doctor was home for Easter Sunday, I continued recording, "Your idea that Carolyn's symptoms are psychological is half baked. Dig deeper for Christ's sake, get a bigger shovel."

She would not sleep another night in this room. We called an ambulance. She fought getting in, like a cat being forced into water.

In a corner her ashes wait in a box, to go to the river.

It's Fall again. Carolyn's son is walking out onto the bridge that joins Bentensport to Vernon township. He throws his mother's remains over the edge. Down river a woman sees something white, the color of rice cakes, swirling, sailing by. She's been out in her yard, beating her rag rugs.

MAKE SOMETHING REAL WITH YOUR HANDS

Damn it, not a cookbook,
a bowl of food.

Outside the soil is delirious
with life. Cumulus clouds, pregnant.
I'm personally afraid to open a window.

Resting in a ripening papaya,
is a Saint's fetus, sucking life.

When the fruit rots and falls
to the ground, a feral cat will eat
one seed. Later he will shit it out
on unkind, rocky roadside soil.
It has the heart to grow right there
and give free food to the poor.

Unless my whole life is a leaking breast,
I am just full of excuses.

LEAVING IOWA

There are drawers full of purple and red
rubber bands,
each one too precious to throw away
after pulling them free of newspapers
or broccoli bundles.

My ball point pens are still
half full of ink.
One of them has a perfect poem
inside it.

Warm wool sweaters, hand knitted
and completely impractical
where I am going,
curl up in my closet
and purr. My leg warmers snarl.

Coming to this country,
we never planned to stay,
never bought anything new
or nice.
Now that we're leaving,
every fork has a name.

TONIGHT SHE IS PRETTY

We visit her deathbed
and wonder what her real name could have been.
Was she always, 'The Midget Hunch Back'?

As a girl, was she so cheerful,
or angry, to be so small and twisted?
No chance to marry or bear a child,
she would have loved a daughter.

Never belonging to a man,
she gave herself to all of us,
until her deformed chest
could no longer hold her swollen heart,
in its cage of bones.

We all agree she's too young
to be dying of huge heart,
though not one of us in this village remembers
the year or day of her unlucky birth.

The men sit outside and talk story softly,
smoking rolled clove cigarettes.

The women brush her high cheekbones
with their lips,
spoon young coconut water
into her cracked mouth
and suffer every last sparrow breath.

CREMATING IBU MANGKU

Your face burning is like a weight on my chest.
I stood beside your son, watching
fire destroy the only you we knew.

You were the woman who would have shared a grandchild
with me, had he lived beyond a few weeks.
Ibu Mangku—Priestess,
diabetic woman who slept until your last day,
with a photo of my daughter, under your pillow.

No matter the heat, the body in death is strong.
For a few moments, engulfed in flame,
you looked like a young number two Balinese wife,
alive, afraid.

The pelvis is the most stubborn part of a woman.
Gasoline fed flames, from two sides, could not destroy
that gateway to Earth.
Your child stood close to the heat,
to stare into the space that opened between worlds
for his particular slipping into life, screaming.

Women should watch their friends being cremated.
It is one way to learn we are made of dust,
organized by breath, water, and heat, into a shape
made for birthing.

THE REDEMPTIONER'S* RECIPE

Julan, you are a daughter of China,
and you are the daughter of a white man.
This is a cadenza you can never reconcile.
All parts are music and noise
seeking painful balance.

If you steal seed
and grow rice, you may return
the harvest.
There is no way to un-harvest a child,
yet you nearly bled to death trying.

What man would demand the fragrant knot of baby
in payment for his seed?
What baby boy would go willingly
away from your voice in two languages,
away from thick yellow-white milk
which only you can make?

Perhaps the heart is a knotted
piece of ginger root.
Asian women often break off a lump
for cooking. Is this what happens
when a baby is born from her body?
Is that child then a broken knot of her,
still fragrant, with hot juicy pulp
like the mother root?

Seems to me the broken place never heals,
it only scars.

> *redemptioner (from the early 17th to 19th centuries) an
> immigrant who obtained passage by becoming an indentured
> servant.—*Random House College Dictionary*

Gina's Hands

Imagine Gina's hands eating popcorn,
gibbon-like fingers would dip
gracefully into the bowl.
Those hands held me tightly
when she birthed her daughters.

Once, on the way to Singapore, we celebrated her birthday
with rose covered chocolate cakes on the airplane.
Chinese New Year, fireworks, chrysanthemum tea.
In the hotel, we deloused all our children.

Chataqua Park, it was autumn in Iowa,
her blue eyes set off the fall colors
and I saw orange, yellow, red, burgundy, even brown... anew.

In the Philippines, she was huge with Eliza
riding upside down under her heart.
There were street lumpias, massages from the blind,
movies for a few pesos and green mango milkshakes.

She ate half her placenta
and took the rest home to plant under a tree in Maine.

Steve, I can remember rushing all over Denpasar
to finish errands, so Gina could get home
in time to make love with you, before boarding the ferry to
Lombok.
When you were in the hospital,
having turned the color of marigolds from malaria,
with no exit visa, how could you be evacuated?
Gina went to every cash machine in Bali,
until she had enough to bribe immigration.
She went bankrupt to save you.
Nearly miscarrying the baby—for not resting, not eating.
She checked every lab report, every medicine you were given.
And all the while she was kind to each nurse,
and person who mopped the hospital floor.

I lied to myself about the tumor, believing it could not be cancer.
Serena's birth on the full moon eclipsed,
we all needed to believe there was no danger of losing Gina.

How can we ever lose Gina,
her smile has infected us forever?

STOOP BERRIES

Grandma Levon and Great Aunt Etha
are no longer able to harvest
the black raspberries.

On the 4th of July in Pleasantville, Iowa,
it's well over 100 degrees out there by the fence.
The tangle and thorns call to the sisters
with finger staining promises
and memories of pies
cut and portioned out decades ago.
Pies that made now dead husbands
lick their fingers
and bear up to the humidity.

This particular year, Levon's grown granddaughter,
Rebecca, braves the berry patch.
She stoops to the lower brambles
where the big berries cluster.
Etha's cinnamon colored cat
teaches her to bend even lower
to where the sweetest fruit hides.
Rebecca leans in farther, thorns catch her blouse.
Looking over her shoulder, she smiles
with purple mouth.
They see her through a pane
of glass and heat ripples
evaporating the day.

When the young woman turns back too quickly,
gets scratched and bleeds,
Levon and Etha touch hands.

ODE TO FRUIT CAKE BAKER

Late in July Edie picks yard pears,
slices and dries them like shriveled moons on wire racks.
By August something signals her to begin saving
the rinds of oranges.
On September first she shops for pecans,
black mission figs, medjool dates from the Holy Land,
a bottle of strong Filipino rum, cherries.

Across the street children assemble
for their first day of school.
She assembles the measuring spoons,
her big blue crockery bowl comes down, she pauses
to consider how old the can of Baking Soda must now be.

The pans are wiped clean and lined
with waxed paper.
Black walnut ground-falls are gathered and cracked.
Flour should be fresh ground. A pinch
of salt brings out the orchid scent of vanilla bean, marries
it to the sugar.
She decides not to blanch the almonds,
a little bitter is good.

He. . . husband, comes home from work
as the cakes emerge from the oven,
helps her pour the dark liquor over,
wraps each one in loosely woven cotton rag.

She posts one to a rural route in Oregon,
another to a P.O. box in Northern California.
The best one goes to the poet.
Listen, to hear the dark
eyes making notes on her cello.
How can the mailman know, on the day before Christmas,

what is so heavy? He drops a white
package on the snowy porch. The poet
will find it in a day, or a week, half buried
half frozen. In her hand she will feel the weight
of being the daughter Edie never had.

WHAT THE FALL BRINGS

When choosing pears,
look to the ground
where the devotees
have already fallen on their knees
in a deep bed of Autumn.
At Point Royal, Pascal's apples are being stolen
away, one moist crumb at a time, by bees.

So many beings walk on water.
Today a snake glided golden
and black striped on the mercury surface
of an Iowa farm pond.
Do the fish look up and see their meter long goddess
flanked by angel dragonflies
humming mantras of mud praise?
Tadpoles offer up
their slick naked skins for her food.
Imagine the light in their eyes, looking up.
The sweet water clams,
hugging the shore, are genuflecting
as she passes; a shadow, a ribbon.

There was an Autumn in France
that inspired a careless conception.
How could a child not wish to become
a mother when the cobbled avenues, stone angels
and painted trees invited life to curl up
in her belly all Winter? That Summer
when the first pain came, the girl remembered
what she'd learned in the Paris Metro;
this going under without fear served her journey
by water and blood to newborn gaze.
Thirty-six years later, she walks the rainy

November streets of her beloved soaking wet city,
looking for traces of the foolish pregnant girl,
who had no centimes for food.

After this life, she plans to take birth
as a wild horse in a mountain valley,
Nepal, or the Lorraine.
If she eats only grass and drinks only water,
her bones will learn to sing.
Her hide-covered flesh will run
until her equine heart breaks diamonds
and the only taste she loves, is wind.

"Aguray" Means Wait

Thunder is never late.
Moments measure distance
from the lightning.
You can count the time between,
the way the midwife counts
your baby *ading's* heart beats,
while mother leans on the walls,
each pain making her pee.

Mortals are always waiting.
Swollen ankles punctuated
by purple want the nine months to end.
So much *aguray.*

Plastic Jesus on the dashboard of a taxi
waits for us to pray.

Like the black dog next door, waiting
to be eaten as *adobo.* Barking keeps the owner
awake all night. In the Philippines,
this is the price of vinegar and dog meat.

Bird song comes before the morning.
The mourning comes before we are ready.
Ay, the barrels are nearly empty,
and so we are waiting for rain.
Sometimes we are waiting to eat food.
In the mountains, we learn this well.
Aguray.

SMOKING IN BAGUIO

After the war years,
Filipino mountain women
would cut off their ear lobes,
ashamed of the big holes
stretched by carnelian trade beads
and iron hoops.
American soldiers don't marry
girls with *Igarot* ears.

This explains why I wear heavy dark silver
and soften my piercings to open wider.
When my holes are huge,
I plan to roll up twenty peso notes,
and stick them through.
A pair of little Filipino flags
waving irreverently
at my American father.

All my life, I've gazed
at the branches of Baguio pines.
God, I wish my mother had hung
my placenta high,
where the birds would come
to eat my angel,
so my flesh could fly away.
But I was born in an American
military hospital.
I lost my placenta.

"We don't do that in our country,"
said the nurse to my *Nanang*
when she, emerging from twilight sleep,
asked to feed me.
Injections were given
to dry up her milk.
I still thirst
and stare at big breasts.

When I get back to the Philippines,
I'm going to let the *Igarot* women
tattoo all the indigo blue mountains on my hands.
I'm going to smoke
a home-grown *cigarillo*
backwards.

Digna stood staring sightlessly on the bridge, holding her baby girl close. Because I knew them well from Project Luke, where I taught, I noticed them in the spaces between the pushing bodies. Baby Aida had just discovered she could crawl.

The wind whipped up from Maharlika Market. Digna turned her face toward it, walked to the concrete edge to smell roasted corn and rotten papayas. Tufts of cloud sitting low against the pillow of the high altitude city drifted by the mother and daughter. On this elevated walkway, planters full of Baguio City flowers separated Filipino pedestrians from the long drop to the busy street below. Digna set Baby Aida down on the narrow planter ledge. Baby Aida was a sighted child.

The blind musicians, busking on the bridge for *centavos* clinking in their tin cans, filled the chilly mountain air with songs of the Holy Season. Baby Aida watched them, because she could. Her hand slapping out the rhythm on her mother's moon face. Her breath making small dragon clouds, which twirled before her black eyebrows and disappeared.

In my classroom I often held and kissed the baby girl. She knew me, with caution and curiosity. However, if I looked directly into her eyes, she would startle backward. The family lived in Barangay Green Water, where only the children could see.

She faced me now, her back to the precipice. Mama Digna hummed to the strains of *"Feliz Navidad,"* her milk white eyes shining. Her arms wrapped around her baby, but so loosely. Aida sat almost still in the planter, her sweater buttoned all the way to the neck. Her hat was red, her eyes huge brown.

I had to do something. My hands ran wet with sweat. My heart twirled in crazy circles, desperate for a scrap of a solution. What, what to do? If I walked toward Baby Aida, our eyes would meet.

"Away in a manger, no crib for his bed, the little Lord Jesus. . . ." My heart rate made a steady climb toward 140. I figured Baby Aida's heart must be working at about 90 to 100 beats per minute. Her heart, only the size of a walnut, inside of her bird's chest.

I prayed for an angel to come, to defrost the moment, and move Digna and the baby away from the edge. I prayed for too long a time. The angels must have been busy with their Christmas shopping. I imagined the baby's guardian angel was buying *lumpias* and *putu* cakes. Why should she hear my plea? Once the baby got to her knees and swiveled to look over the edge, she smiled at the dented yellow and blue cabs and jangling hot pink jeepneys flashing by under her perch.

A decision to walk away came to me like a whisper of wind around my left ear: *Trust the blind mother, she knows her world better than you do, sister.* I was trembling as I ran down the cement steps to the level of the street. I knocked over a lazy angel, who was begging at the bottom. I stood between traffic lanes, below Baby Aida for a long time, smelling the diesel and imagining she was safe.

Monday morning as I entered the classroom at Project Luke, my heart leapt. My arms reached for Baby Aida. The moment she met my seeing eyes, Aida rappelled off her mother and tumbled to the wooden floor.

A CIRCLE FOR PUTU

If I had inscribed a circle around her,
a circle of dragonflies,
a circle of prayers,
a circle more protective than love,
would she still be alive?
Will I ever stop doing the mental postmortem?

She was the baby girl next door,
obsidian eyes,
just learning to question.

There are memories I must drive away;
Putu's dancing feet on my kitchen table.
Her one toe, twisted over the other.
How she looked in my granddaughter's
hand-me-down dresses.
The shine of her black hair
when I picked lice from her head.
My son's voice, speaking to her so softly.

Would her mother's milk have saved her?
She was doomed to drink from a bottle,
while her young mother dripped tears and white milk.
This is an Indonesian story, often told.

Was she cheated?
Is it true that people do not die
before their time?
Is there a clock on God's wall
where each of us has a birthday,
and a death day?

If so, why does a circle of owls
all wearing Putu's eyes,
follow me in dreams?

THE MIDWIFE'S APPETITE

This dawn rain soothes and washes.
Having spent another night
wrapped in the blanket of insomnia
the province of owls and midwives,
I need the rain
like I need the scent of your body
sleeping beside me. It is a kind of food.

Often I come home, having spent most of the night
between the legs of birth.
That door where we women tear and bite at angel's wings,
where birth and death embrace and make a kind of peace.

You are waiting in the pillows
strewn with fallen hair.
Without waking, you put your arms around me.
You know where I've been.
You can smell the blood and salty water
that no shower could really wash away.

Our son keeps a snake
who sheds his milky skin
and emerges like a Phoenix—
his body all the colors of fire and rainbow.
After each rebirth, he is hungry
and eats rats.

When we bathe in salty sweat
reborn by breath and the drive to join bodies,
I fly up from the blankets and pillows
like the Phoenix. I am so hungry.

VICTIMS OF HUMAN

I am slicing apples
in a cinnamon dream.
It is that time of year; Even in Indonesia,
our Muslim and Hindu friends come to break bread.

As we string lights,
I am bent with remembering
my first terrorist Christmas.

Father was in Vietnam;
he sent a small box.
Sleeping inside was the scent of Quin Yon
and the most beautiful doll. Her glass eyes
stared at me from that land
where my father was trapped between politicians,
words and bullets.
She wore a scarlet dress, high in the neck, down to her toes,
slit on the sides, where her long silk pants could be seen.
In her wide rice straw hat she appeared
to be twelve years old, like me. Her breasts were a firm promise.
I knew her father was also in the war, and could die.

When I turned her over, her back was sliced open
straw and Asian newspaper oozing out - dried doll blood.
I cried, "Who would do this?"
Tenderly my mother explained, "In times of war
the police and government must break everything open
to see if a bomb is inside."
Mother knew about war,
having been a small Filipino girl in WWII.

I loved my torn-open Vietnamese doll, more than any other.
I refused to give her a name,
she was every girl on Earth.

> *"We believe there is hope for humans to behave humanely."*
> —Lucy Wisdom, Sumatran Orangutan Society

Mary's Quilt

Mary gave three people bodies of breath and blood,
after carrying them in the boat
of her burgundy womb.
This fleshy ship of souls, now cut away.

Gone the beautiful lips of Mary's cervix.
Gone too, the secret cervical crypts
who watered the kisses
her husband so loved to taste.

It began with making love
and a flood of blood.
The tests proved danger,
proved she had cancer.
Aggressive, primitive rogue cells
in all her sacred, hidden places.

After the cutting,
scarlet and purple essential parts of her scattered.
Where are the glistening almond ovaries,
carrying the oocytes
of four hundred thousand potential babies?
Mary was born with these babies inside her.

What if we women dream,
not with our brains, not with our hearts,
but with our wombs?
What if we make the whole world
anew each night, patched-up and reborn,
from the slippery waters and blood of our baby houses?

Can all the hot ironing
by masked doctors
really stop the cancer?

Can we women weave the world
when so many of our sisters
have lost their dreaming jewel ovaries,
red wombs. . . ships of secrets?

Can we stitch all the torn dream patches together
to make a quilt sewn with the long strands
of Mary's fallen hair?

MY DAUGHTER'S BRIDE PRICE

"Deja, it's times like these . . . stillness engulfs me, and nothing else matters,
except living! I thank Ja for this beautiful life, where I'm assured that in
some corner of the world, you are in it."
 —Dumisani Dlamini
 text message sent just hours
 before he was shot in his home in South Africa

He would come here,
make his first trip to Asia,
to ask my daughter's *lobola*—her bride price.

He would offer his heart, carved of plum colored hope,
and all the images he captured on film,
to change a world, to heal a country—
one pair of eyes at a time.

A phone call at four in the morning
peels the skin from my child.
She will be homesick forever.
Her eyes will dart to every corner of every room
she enters, will search at every airport and station
for him.

A mother mourns her daughter's murdered dreams,
and bends to cry over unconceived grandchildren.
The media says the violence in South Africa
is worsening—all are punished. All are punished.

My bride price, for this astonishing soul,
wrapped in a body that bled from mine,
first born flower of fools,
bone of ancient family bones,
is dear.

I want two bullets.

Two bullets never made,
never sold.
Two bullets never bought by murderers,
never loaded, never fired.

Zhòuie's Dream

She feels warm,
as if fever were coming.
She rolls toward me in the bruised light
of second morning New Year in Bali.
"I miss you even when you're right here."

I know what this means.
Know her bones will ache for impossible union.
Her heart must unlatch
painfully as a peony,
who lets the ants eat her face off,
so that she may crack open and blossom.

She's not yet reached seven years,
but her Buddha vows. . . to love and love and love,
already bruise her brown feet.

I am only the *Lola*, the grand mothering one,
so I lay a hand on her back and lie,
"It's O.K."

Her breath is nutmeg and sandalwood scented,
it takes me down to another dream,
a weaving of owl wings,
a massage by spider's hands.

A drumming Indonesian earthquake
jolts and rolls the bed.
My granddaughter sleeps on,
for at least a small while.

You Ask How a Midwife is Made

First a girl has a daughter,
a being born when a sparrow and a sea turtle
mate impossibly.
No manger to lay down in, this child comes silently
before dawn lights the little trailer in a garden by the tracks.
Too poor to imagine poverty, the baby feeds
on the cracked, sore nipples of love, while hummingbirds
and crickets sing in the sunflower and sweet pea teepee.

As the girl rolls her baby in autumn leaves
dioxins kill babies in Italy. Boats full of refugees
are sunk by governments. Oil becomes more precious
than the weight of a human or owl's soul.

A slow revolution and six more babies
woke her up to the truth,
that she cannot protect her seven children or the owls
unless she takes the yellow dress her Filipino
grandmother offers her in a dream.

This tattered yellow garment becomes a flag of peace.
It signals a war will be fought with the weapons of gentle love,
and a trembling hand to give comfort.
She cannot change this world, where shadow puppets
dance on the red lips of volcanoes,
and miracles are extinct,
but she must bend to her work.

What to Say to My Friend's Husband When He Cheats

Who is it that you imagine you are,
separate from God,
who can cheat or be cheated?

There are little symbols of love
everywhere we look
and forget to look.
See how the Papaya is scarred
by each fallen leaf and fruit—every scar
in the shape of a heart.

Yet we are orphans.

Breaking her heart open
does not make you a demon,
an angel,
a hero,
or a cad.

You are just another tool of impermanence,
a puppet of fate, with a hard-on for himself
in the mirror of a new woman.

Once a skin puppet held up to her light,
you made a beautiful shadow.
Now you have broken the lamp
and cry invisibly in the dark.

Banjo Zoo

When every dark afternoon
could bring an earthquake or a newborn child,
your feet carry your body
like a pair of married turtles.
They navigate the sea of cups of coffee, motorbikes,
picking up passports, drinking young coconuts
and buying street food from refugees.

Turtles can move slowly through the garden of red ginger,
or fly up the bamboo stairs.
Eventually,
they guide you home from your work in Sulawesi or Borneo
to play the banjo.

Some nights the turtles
crawl to my side of the bed.
They are cold,
having shed the shell of the day.

The turtles have already woken the
dove winged hands, and all the animals
that live in your skin zoo—
blue butterflies, black monkeys, and coiling reptiles.

Dancing together as they do
always makes the ocean crave salt,
The sun may even switch on a lamp.

LOSING BABY TABITHA

At one point five kilograms,
you are too damn small to breathe.
Being proud and stupid and well trained,
I breathe for you, an hour, more. . . .
Your Sumbanese heart, size of penny, broken by poverty
beats a little faster, giving me a rotten egg of hope.

You open black eyes and see me bent over.
Feel my fingers on your heart, forcing a beat as gently as I can.
Feel my mouth over your face, desperate kisses.
You blink, a response, and stare in disbelief.
Is this LOVE? Your eyes ask.
And I know it is not really love, it is the midwife's habit.
It is the oath to protect life—for I really do fear death.
Almost every person you could meet, here on Earth, fears death.
If you would just breathe with me, and then breathe on your own. . .
You could grow a while, and learn to also fear death.

But Tabitha, you are not buying any of it—not the breathing
                                nor the muscle tone
                                    no color of pink life
                                        and finally, no heartbeat.
Do you want me to stop?
I stop. All the angels in the room exhale, and just leave you alone.
Having read the braille of your face, I won't cry at your grave.

Infant CPR

I have shaved God's head and forged
the hum of bees,
to breathe life into a flaccid born baby,
to trade a few years of my own time,
a bargain if this one
gasps and lives.

She will grow now and dance in a Hindu temple,
and make a shape against
the Balinese sky.
Long after I am resting in ash, one may trace her shadow.

The puppet master called me to her birth.

For Lakota

There was one perfect day,
when your mom, Brenda, and I walked, heavy
with your brothers under our belly-drums.
Each boy kicked mightily in the cages of our ribs.

It was Hawaii, you were three years old and fond
of salty foods dipped in yogurt.
Your hair was a tangle, you would not tolerate the comb.

Brenda brought a foil wrapped treasure of dark Swiss chocolate.
She opened it in a pineapple field.
The rows rolled away from where we sat, spinney,
dusty green fruit, gliding all the way over
the hills, celadon stripes to the sea.

You were small, and in less than two years
Brenda would die.

Today we celebrate your twenty-forth birthday.
In adolescence you worried that you might
forget Brenda's face.

I began to cling to each memory of her.
I wove webs around each story, and smile.
Why are there so few photos?

The chocolate was biter sweet.
I am still holding that perfect day in my mouth.
I am certain you can taste it.

—July, 2010

64

A SMALL WHITE FEATHER

For Marilyn Hacker and Hanifa

The last dream of dawn was of my lover stroking my clitoris,
with a small white feather.
Is that how we left it when I ran off sometime between
three and four a.m. to deliver a baby?

The baby, an Islamic girl,
ink black eyes and black curls she will hide under a lovely veil.
Hide from whom?
When they leave the clinic today,
I will tell her father that I have already circumcised her.
He will praise my efficiency.
Her mother will know I have lied.
A woman's secret need never be discussed.

My closest neighbor wears the *krudung*,
I love her.
She names her new daughter Hanifa Isthara Sabiza.
A name must be a poem.

In the batik shop I saw you poet, missing a breast.
I wanted to touch you there, and move my hands
from full side to scar, living under the blue motif.
I held back, you didn't mind my imagined caress.
In a more honest lifetime, I will touch you for real.

In the land I half belong to,
children are taught to fear Muslims.
It's a damn deep scar.

Mohamed told the desert men never to bury
their newborn daughters alive. . . .
This was common, a man's responsibility.
A strong man never talks of the small perfect hand
that squeezed his finger as the sand enveloped the bright new soul.

He knows it takes courage to do his duty; the girl facing the sky,
her black hair, black eyes shining one last moment in the hot day.
All these ages later, I realize that Mohamed was a deviate.
Imagine him saying that in war,
      men may not kill:
      women, children, elders or trees.
The last dream of dawn—my lover.
A small white feather. A child.

                                  —Sept. 11. 2007

Left in a Room Somewhere

Is a herd of butterflies
born from my heart, at the moment
of your first touch on my skin.

They followed you more than seventeen years,
into the river to swim,
onto airplanes bound for Sarawak, Kalimantan, South Jersey.
Every purple and red creature in the herd
beat its dusty wings fast and faster
to keep up with you on the motorbike.

I am amazed that other men
did not see them follow you into public bathrooms.
You took them to work with your sound equipment.
I suspect our children sensed them pulsing all about you
when you returned home.

Perhaps they fed on the oil of your skin,
or the odors of our lovemaking
which made them glow
like lightening bugs.

Last August
in a room somewhere. . .
you entered clothed in all my butterflies,
and left naked.

I dreamed I wrote you a love note
or tried to write, on the surface of a beaten egg.
All the viscous broken yellow
swallowed the meaning.

Normally, I never asked you what to do
to fix tears between us,
we had the butterflies to do that.

JANET'S SON HAS DIED

We live on opposite sides of the earth
yet, sad news travels like heat lightning,
Janet, your son has died today.
I don't know how, or why he died,
only that he has gone from the seasons of your sturdy
Midwestern home, forever.

In my Indonesian kitchen, tomatoes are still ripening.
It is impossible to understand how.
How natural processes just keep unfolding after
Daniel has died in Iowa.
The trees in the backyard will miss him.
The squirrels stealing nuts, will miss him.
The snow, come winter, will miss him.

We women, who have had enough years to stop ripening
the eggs in our ovaries, enough years to learn to love each
other so gracefully, must bend with your grief.

I remember him only as a tall teenager, how he shyly shook my hand
when I met him in the kitchen. There were bananas
on the counter that morning.

Daniel helped your husband teach my sons magic.
That spring he opened a world of all-possibilities to the younger boys.
Gently he pried the doors of their imaginations ajar,
and my sons still have a bit of stardust at their fingertips.

My daughter, but a year younger than Dan, has finished
college, and she is confused about her future,
Her spirit feels paralyzed. I can't promise her
that it will get any less confusing on this planet.

I wish I could promise her that young people will never
die. That friends will not need to light candles for the loss.
I must tell her, that some evenings,
our bedtime tea, will taste of tears.

ZHÒU'S JOURNEY

I dreamed you
    stood on a river bank at Varanasi,
    all of the floating candles offered there, fell in love with your flame.

You were sick in a dark hotel room in Rishikesh,
wondering why the chai in India did not compare to
the spiced tea you grew up on.

Turned away at an ashram in Dharmasala: "No Visitors Allowed,"
you began to truly miss home.

Dusty trains enveloped you in poverty and smeared you with noise.
At the Ganges you found incense pots, mud flowers,
the living and the dead taking baths together.
There was song and marigold color for comfort.

Twenty-three years ago I noticed you had arrived quietly.
Hiding in the purple place, deep inside of me.
You grew there, first a butterfly, a fish, a swan, an entire
ox rolling over to look at the moonrise.
In increments you filled the place behind my heart. And,
instead of going to India that year, I birthed you.

Today you return home, and give me a Tibetan coat,
black and stitched with rainbows, like your hair in sunshine.
Your eyes share a story, more radiant than all the dreams
I ever had of that lost journey, and I could not be more pleased
to have stayed home.

PUSHES

You were born with sweating
horses inside of you.
Stars died at that moment
to enter your soul,
and petal-by-petal a new flower invented
a salt kind of rain.

Your father wanted a good son.

The second hurt:
A redwood tree pierced your center
on it's way to pushing
your mind God-ward.
You drew this in pencil, once.
When glands awoke,
it was too much.
And then, grandfather died of AIDS.

The third push:
You call it dropping-out,
running away, quitting,
when at age sixteen you stalk
your father,
never putting more than twenty miles of space
between you, and his barricade.
It's an elliptical orbit,
when you draw near him, he moves away.

Sweat your horses.
Rain your star odor on his house,
until he has formaldehyde
in his eyes.
You were not born to be his acceptable boy.
You may teach your father redwoods.

Someday your own son will be named for a tree.

ODE TO DRY STARLIGHT

Today I saw a galaxy behind my dream.
Many million pinpoints of light
bled through my eyelids, in the newborn day.

I can't be sure if this beauty
was due to my over fifty years of seeing,
or perhaps all the stardust and vernix from the babies
I have received, has been rubbed roughly
by my hands into my eyes.
Eyes so tired and scratched.
Eyes open to see a fifteen-year-old girl
push an unwanted baby into our world of noise
and light, and die.

When I was twenty-seven, invincible
still insulated by health and energy,
a dying father said to me, "Enlightenment is nothing
more than accepting the unacceptable."

I did not cry for the girl or her baby.
Enlightenment is a drying up and hardening
of the eyes.

SEXING THE HUMAN

"Poetry is the journal of a sea animal living on land, wanting to fly in the air."
—Carl Sandburg

The mind is a simian, a monkey thing.
A primate: a mammal of an order
that includes the lemurs, bush babies,
tarsiers, marmosets, monkeys, apes, and humans.
They are distinguished by having hand like feet,
and forward-facing eyes,
and, with the exception of humans,
are typically agile tree-dwellers.

The chemical-hormonal aspects of the mind
are just too exhaustive to understand,
but as an animal, I know him well.
He sleeps at night, even when he feels guilty.

Mind can take us anywhere he wants—
to libraries or slums of prostitution.

Swan, the heart, does not necessarily
want to go along with the monkey mind.
She prefers small servings of lovely foods.
She paints with a pastel rainbow.

The soul, who perhaps is the androgynous one in the trilogy,
(mine is a Pegasus) tries to steer the body-vehicle
but is not always successful.
And so, people have car-wreck lives.

About the soul. . . You can't keep it, it keeps you.

Free will is a rabid dog who was once an adorable puppy.

THE SHORT ENCYCLOPEDIA OF READING:
PREFERRING SKY, MOUNTAINS, SINGING PLANTS AND SMALL ANIMALS

Poem 1

It makes absolutely no sense who
we humans give our lives to.

My daughter is a Mahatma,
a soul born shiny and true.
The man who undoubtedly loves her
accuses her of infidelities she never imagined.
He is using a fly-swatter kind of love,
to catch a hummingbird's soul.

Hummingbirds live only a few seasons,
all of them outdoors.
The only way to catch a bird
who can never stop trembling,
is to stand still and emit the odor of pollen,
or kiss with the flavor of passion fruit nectar.

This man has a heart like deep space,
full of stars, exploding heat, and ice.
He does not know that a trapped hummingbird
can starve to death in an hour,
or that her blue throated
heart beats 1,260 times per minute.

Poem 2

Prisms need incident light to
send color, they don't make rainbows alone.
Perhaps this explains why
I become invisible
When you stand too far away.

Poem 3

The apparent color of each hummingbird
depends upon microscopic distances between
ridges in her feathers.
Making her up with pigment
will do nothing to improve upon her
iridescent beauty.

Poem 4

When suturing a woman's yoni
torn by childbirth
all the colors of hummingbirds,
and their music,
may fly into your mind.
This should not interfere
with the repair of lotus or human flesh.

Poem 5

On a good day the woman giving birth
has a husband
who has not been committed
to an Indonesian insane asylum,
for speaking to the dead and inventing new colors
for hummingbirds.

FOR ALEXANDER LANGER FROM A MIDWIFE

If only you were on this very train to Verona,
I could lean forward and put half my music into your left ear.
Maybe, from where your soul stays,
you can you hear the small voice of violin bringing guitar
to his knees in gratitude, in harmony.
Politely, I would avoid your eyes,
ringed in purple exhaustion,
and focus my gaze
on the windows streaked with metallic sky-tears.
The farmers of your country have ploughed
the Italian earth for Autumn.
This black soil will receive the snow soon,
had you lived, your hair would be white by now.

In my dream, you held me with what felt
like acceptance, something no father and no lover ever offered.
Sunburned angel, you kissed the sorrows from my head.

My book, in Italian language, is the child
of your dream of peace
mated with my love for women.

I want to wear a t-shirt
with your sorrowful face printed on it.
A tattoo,
a shroud of political Turin.

The land you loved opens to receive
the birth blood of women, which I dilute
with wash-water and sweat.
You would have thought me young,
yet, I have grandchildren.
I ask my generations
to carry your satchel
and walk in your sandals.

Mentored by the dead
traveling a train of desire in a man's name,
listening to the cadence of a voice I never heard.
Is this guidance by a saint or sinner's soul?
I can never prove what I feel, except in a dance
I am too shy to move with.

If I am to speak your words of peace,
must I eat your sorrow?
And Alexander, must you chew
life's food with my mouth?

Did your promise of compassion burn
you to madness?
Or, did you plan all these days,
after taking your own life,
to become the sum of so many pilgrims
born gently into my ugly hands?
Your memory infects hearts,
and grows roots to my feet.

What would you like for dinner Alex—
A dried cherry, a cocoa bean, or a lamb of God?
I would sacrifice much to have known you a little.

Kneeling witness at the birth bed of Indonesia's poverty,
High Priestess of blood and sparrow wings
broken by the windstorms of conflict,
one war pretends to end and another begins.
I imagine they who loved you so,
buried you in a box of roses,
but I was not there to see.

I missed you.
I miss you.

After the funeral
your friends paired off
to drink the pale wine of body fluids,
to scream in the silence of sated cells,
"I am yet alive! Alive!"
You cried for every boy sacrificed in hatred
and every girl raped by soldiers.
Was it not a violence you did to your own body?
A violence on each of us, forever shocked
into loving without compromise.
One of your lovers became a law-maker,
another a priest.
All of them midwife the stillbirth
of a difficult peace.

Another Autumn passes and ploughs
Summer's dances and fine dreams
into stained yellow newspaper clippings.

We are all endangered
yet, somehow we drink red wine
and eat warm chestnuts
knowing tomorrow's menu
is only atomic wind.

Forgive me for writing it too honestly—
as I have allowed your words to escape my blue lips.
May I ask you, did you ever become who you wanted to be?

—Autumn 2007

77

TSUNAMI NOTEBOOK

poems washed up from the sea of tears

Robin Lim 2005

Have you wondered why all the windows in heaven were broken?

Have you seen the homeless in the open grave of God's Hand?

—Kenneth Patchen

To Love a Wife

Bang Hanafi had a wife. She visited his leaf-enhanced dreams
to tell him where to find their baby daughter. She told him to dig
under a tree, by a shaft of sunlight, where she and the baby were
waiting.

He led his few friends with picks, and an old shovel, to the deep mud.

When she was uncovered, he said she was beautiful.
"In her life she was black and thin. She had wished to be
plump and white, and now she has grown big, pale.
"I only wish I had some fragrant oil, to help her smell a little better."

Notes Taken Flying Low and Slow on a Red Cross Plane

First the earthquake,
and the women trying to save their kitchen glass.
The men regretted their broken aquariums,
tenderly, they lifted the fish into plastic bowls for safety.

There were some minutes of peace.
The mothers serving morning rice.
Sunday market bustling.
The sea receded and the prices dropped
as old men walked out to pick fish
like fallen fruit around the feet of trees in season.
While chewing and haggling the people heard the ocean explode.
Explode like a bomb.
Then he, Neptune, or some bastard adolescent son of the sea god
began to roar.

He came as a hot black wall,
stinking breath,
white cobra teeth.

Tsunami, we later called him,
came from many directions,
pushing trees, buildings, cars, mothers, cousins,
babies, wooden cabinets—full of everything we had,
many kilometers inland.

The scrap metal that cut
Rizky's cheek
decapitated his father.
Rizky, eight orbits old,
let go of his father's body and found a wooden plank
which carried him upcountry in the flood.
His cousin floated on an upholstered couch in comfort,
but it was sucked back out to sea. Gone.

81

Sarjani's six year old daughter was torn
from her arms.
All the mothers repeat and repeat the story,
of not holding onto the baby.
A carabao offered her horn
and swam to the surface. An old cow
dragging a pregnant woman skyward,
to leave her by the roof of the *Masjid*.
She gave birth that evening, right on the tin roof of that Mosque.
Seventy people found refuge there,
imagine that one would be a birthing woman,
another a midwife.
When the water receded, they lowered the baby down
in a black plastic bag.

In the rubber forest you will find "Search and Rescue"
workers, and survivors. Everyday they look for people;
after two months they still find fifteen bodies, twenty bodies,
everyday. They don't worry about where to dig, wherever they dig,
bones and a little flesh, torn garments to be recognized,
wait to be found. Why do people wait for prayers?
     The animals, those not in cages,
     quietly walked upcountry, when the earthquake began.
     Somehow they expected the sea to be drunk with anger,
     and so they left.

ROTI ACEH

They call this bread. . . *roti,*
spun from precious sugar,
boiled in coconut milk,
pounded from rice,
woven with hands which swam the tsunami waters
and somehow lived.
And somehow, painted red with henna, remember how to cook.

The veiled women send this 'bread of Aceh,'
like skeins of golden cord, tightening
around my life.
It pulls me back to the clinic,
to unhealed wounds,
unattended sorrows,
merciless dreams of remembering baby daughters.

This sweetened thread loaf
ties me to sleep, on hard packed Sumatran sand
where hundreds of thousands of recently dead souls
are also trying to sleep.

The women, picking seaweed from their black hair,
packed this witch-bread in a box of prayers,
heaven's banquet labeled: Operation Blessing.

Losing Trust in the Rainbow

He is my most musical child,
this, last one from my body—
copper, copper, red, pink, rusty penny boy.
He is the child of the truest and unexpected
love of my life.
The love that rings in the bells of my body
and wakes me like an earthquake,
spills like water
from one flooded rice field to all the fields
freshly planted below.
A spreading deep green glass floor
reflecting storms.

In Aceh, I saw the end of the world.
The rainbow promise of a senile God, broken.
We can never fix it, or mend even one sorrow
by sharing grief or forgiving ourselves for still living.
Enough,
the bird still sings and I pray for my own children.

WHAT WILL NEVER DRY

On the beach at Melabouh,
fifty-four days after the tsunami,
I found a seaman's hat
just coming ashore, home without the sailor.
Two twisted tricycles,
plastic torn from soup packages,
a little bit of hand crocheted shawl,
a boy's shoe, size seven, with no sole.
a hermit crab, living in a perfect shell.
a rusty broken military tower looking west.
The sun is setting upon a peaceful glass table-top
green and silver sea.

Behind me is a mass grave and a Mosque still standing.
God, what does that mean? In nearly every village
and broken seaside city, the arched Mosques
with onion shaped copper crowns, still gleam in the day,
stand proud and mostly white.
The Indian Ocean tenderly sprays my face with his salty spit.
I am aroused by his breath in my ears, and so I walk forward a step
until I am wet.
He is warm, the temperature of tears.

ARTIFACTS OF DEATH

My beautiful son, baked black
home from the tsunami waters
where he and his brother, and some old farts
towed donated fishing boats
to villages who lost all.
They had 300 boats,
but they need only one now
because they lost most of their people.
The dead don't eat fish.
Quite the opposite. . . .

Thor shows me a collection, gifts from Acehnese survivors;
an old war bayonet, used to kill many rebels.
His sweaty hand opens to show me tiger's teeth.
He unfolds a plastic body bag, sees my eyes
and says, "Don't worry mom, it's never been used."

I send my sons to Aceh; this is their school,
"Earthquake High,"
where the sea eats everything loved.

The Buddha sat under a tree, attacked by his own
fear of death,
or fear of life,
until every sword that pierced his heart
became a flower.
He had it easy.
I immerse my children in annihilation.
They come home to show me what remains.
Is the heart indestructible?
Or, do we burnish it shiny, to the density of stone?
What kind of mother have I become?
I give them bitter learning and cruel medicine.
They come home and hug me.

ACEH LULLABY FOR SLEEPING ALONE

Our lives are sewn
together with a long and painful needle,
the thread pulls—catches our flesh,
tears.

We grow older chasing prayers
at night, at high speed
on the saddle of
a motorcycle, in the rain.

Prayers said in dangerous languages,
without words, or mouths
to speak them.

Tonight, I forded a river, with a bleeding woman
on a stretcher. It was cold, and I thought of your eyes
to give me courage.

Your eyes are a December sky in Sumatra.
Mine are average, brown.

Peace, is the weight of your body odor
taking me down
to dream, with the starfish.

Peace, is your voice weaving
a story, for our son's pillow.

Peace, is the clay colored wing
of the monkey bird, as I describe
him to you over the satellite phone, and you
see him alive in my syllables, exactly.

Murni Dead and Cremated

Imagine life without the shine of those blackest eyes,
and my eyes must look and look at her painting.
Her fantasy, a flying carpet, a protozoan angel
eating a woman's yoni upside down, like a fetus.
My God, the carpet is sprouting rice.

News of Murni gone, sends me up the water tower,
a dangerous windy place to cry.

First comes a yellow honey sipping bird,
I am hugging my knees, rocking, asking for signs—
Did she die before her time?
Is this place, where the rubber slippers
and skulls of children were washed ashore,
right for a clinic?
My grief and my work all mixed up.
This is how a woman named for a bird must cope.

Then she comes, lifting off the slow river
like an ancestral shadow, the Great Blue Heron.
If I could know all the blood I carry, all the cultures
that sent their sons and daughters out to make me,
all of them would have worshiped this bird.

She circles twice and leaves me asking
the next and the next question.
How can I cry now? And then. . .
a pair of blazing kingfishers dives and rolls
and alights on a branch of thinnest bamboo
to share a meal of minnow.
Rain and tears in Aceh, are equally torrential.

Murni's hand will never move to paint this.

WASHING UP THE TSUNAMI

Not at all like wringing
out panties in the sink,
this is laundry.
Washing sheets a paralyzed boy
has peed on.
No machine here,
only a deep well of tangy metallic water
and my rough hands,
under a huge hot sky, and
I love it.

Where we wash in Aceh
is a place poems are born
and fly away before words are pinned to them.

Walking to the clothesline
cobras twist to show me the way.
My steps are taken with goat's hooves.
I glide through grass and dune weed,
sand and swamp mud between cloven
toes that know where to step to avoid human remains.
Yes, this is where people washed up
last December, without their souls.

The West coast of Aceh,
where this clinic rests on a shaky point,
is like a vat of darkest red dye,
where I am dipped.
Each time under I come out darker
and mordant this color of Sumatran shade
with hammered loneliness.

—Aceh Barat, January 2006

The Tao of Disaster

TRAVELING TO HAITI

Triage: To separate out,
assess the wounds of battle,
assign degrees of urgency,
when the numbers are too many.

We do this to bodies.
Eventually, we do it to souls. . .
". . .too much damage to salvage this one."

Perhaps the capacity to cope
has been impaired beyond human repair.
There are too many ways to describe pain
in our vocabulary.

Those in the middle,
with wounds, but not so deep,
those who can still walk unassisted,
seek someone more unharmed to love.

—Jan. 2010

Sunday in Haiti

"Glory, glory. . . " the people sing,
salvation songs poured out from their cracked
hearts. Songs more lovely, blue and red
from the heart of the palm of Haiti's flag,
flown in French Creole harmonies.

Those with broken legs pray for crutches.
Some rejoice with one arm missing,
"Hallelujah, hallelujah. . ." sing the homeless,
and "Thank you, for I am saved
by the blood of Jesus from the grave
of cement falling mercilessly from above."

Cement without steel reinforcement
and too much sand;
engineered to save money, not souls.

Praise and gratitude, rings in the streets of
Jacmel and
the falling down churches of Port-au-Prince.
How can we keep from crying?

Where is the song of the orphaned child?
Screamed in silences from their eyes,
three reverent, solemn, sacred words,
"Why? Why? Why?"

                              —Feb. 2010

HAITI IS

It is said Haiti is the poorest country in the Western hemisphere.
        I saw Haiti. . .
Haiti is a broken Digicell hand-phone in every tight jean pocket.
Haiti is an emaciated black brindled goat, with one broken horn.
Haiti is a snake with two heads.
Haiti is a hungry nine-year-old boy balanced
        on the fender of a tap-tap, begging for water.
Haiti is a shaved Samson.
Haiti is a line at the airport, relatives leaving for anywhere.
Haiti is a garage sale.
Haiti is a child-beating, "You look just like your father!"
Haiti is a Port-au-Prince barbeque, with four million guests,
        and only twenty-two chicken legs to grill.
Haiti is a tent city with no tents.
Haiti is a loud radio station playing love songs on a dusty day.
Haiti is a passel of sway-back pigs eating medical waste.
Haiti is a rainbow bus with Jesus painted on the back to redeem us.
Haiti is an argument in French-Creole.
Haiti is a baby boy named Lovenski and a little girl called Divine
        Blessing.
Haiti is Osana and Hallelujah, and pray for me, but for God's sake,
        give me water.
Haiti is a big gorgeous black woman in a red dress,
        who refuses to straighten her hair.
Haiti is expecting another baby.
Haiti is expecting another earthquake.
Haiti is expecting hurricane season.
Haiti is the sweetest funeral song.
Haiti is a turquoise wave breaking against a lime white cliff.
Haiti is a wooden house built in 1878 from beached pirate ships,
        that stands when all the pretty cement houses have fallen.

Haiti is a tin roof "bang" when a mango falls,
     the neighbors are happy it's not gunshot.
Haiti is a premature baby in a hospital bucket.
Haiti is a brass band of old men in uniforms, walking home from
     the graveyard.
Haiti is a mosquito infecting a widow with dengue fever.
Haiti is four million kids with scabies.
Haiti is a queer expat artist, dead under the rubble,
     while still young and beautiful.
Haiti is a voodoo priest down every Catholic alley.
Haiti is a Jesus song.
Haiti is 300,000 child slaves.
Haiti is 40% of the population under fourteen years of age,
     10% will die before they are five.
Haiti is a Spanish nun sweating in the sun.
Haiti is an orphaned nation.
Haiti is a child named Whiskey.
Haiti is fighting a virus.
Haiti is a gentle lover, a jealous lover.
Haiti is a twenty-two year old Canadian soldier with a gun and a stick.
Haiti is the tears of a man with four small children,
     burying his wife and newborn baby girl.
Haiti is a tired donkey loaded down with sweet mandarin oranges
     for market.
Haiti is a corn and coconut fritter, one of millions, made with
     loving black hands.
Haiti is a mother, braiding her small daughter's hair with rainbow
     ribbons.
Haiti is pregnant with hope.

—Feb. 2010

WHY WAR TOYS SELL LIKE HOTCAKES

I keep reading poems,
never finding in them a word
about circumcision.

No one wants to talk
about the circumstraint board,
the scalpel,
or the scream.
The sound that sears through
an infant boy's first erection.

Where the hell
is his mother?

After a thousand nerves
are severed,
amputation complete,
does the boy, now unconscious,
believe that mother has disappeared?
How long is forever
in that sleep punctuated with shudders, sobs?
What have they done with his foreskin?

Lying in a flooded rice paddy,
smelling his own legs rotting
in the mud,
a boy wonders, *Why did I sign up for this war?*
He drifts back to the day of his birth.

Oh yeah, you do this going back thing
when you die.
A man wearing a mask
is quick about his work.
Cold, hard beneath the baby. Straps
hold him absolutely still. Lights blinding.
Sounds shattering the clean of steel.
Where is the warm one, the muffled voice, the mothering thing?
What is the signal
for no?
Please don't hurt me!

At the very last
he recalls feeling this:
I don't, I won't need anyone, never.

Imagine now, all the foreskins
quilted together.
It would make an enormous flag.
We could fly it above our painful lives.
Stretched high, so no sun could warm us.
No rain would water our crops.
What would we call this country?

HUMANE MEANS WOMAN

Mangoes are much like men.
The hairy ones, blemished on the outside,
that leave you picking your teeth after the feast,
are often the sweetest.

My mother would reach for perfection
while Filipino *Lola*, she would roll her eyes
at the Baguio market
and choose bruised fruit.

I had only thought she was frugal
and learned over these fifty-four years,
my grandmother was wise.

When the Buddha took life as King of the Monkeys,
he ordered his prehensile tailed subjects
to pluck every golden mango
from the river,
before they could be tumbled down
to the Empire of men.
Once, a fruit escaped, floated downstream,

rolled in a lazy eddy,
rode on white water rapids,
found it's way all the way downriver,
until it was tasted by men.
Delighted, drunk on flavor as blinding as the sun,
the Emperor ordered an army to capture the monkey lands
and kill the simian lords and ladies of the mango trees.

This is the price of sweet, the price of golden flesh.

As I said. . . men are like mangoes. And, they like mangoes.

Now, dragons in the East, were beneficent and bestowed fertility.
While they inhabited the earth, they breathed fire,
plunged into the seas with ease, and navigated
the heavens on great wings.
Dragons could not tolerate lies,
so they spoke only with women.

Today, men say dragons and Buddha monkeys are mythical,
but women remember and know many truths.

THE CHANCE TO OWN HER HISTORY

—For Marjorie Evasco

Was I cold in adolescence
or just feeling my dead *Lola*?

I felt the pain of the *anting-anting* she put under my skin
one stormy night in Baguio.
Baguio the name that means typhoon,
hometown of my own true mother.

Lola's hands were already ancient,
many years before I took birth.
Hands, gnarled and twisted from the sick she healed,
and the babies she received to earth
now already grown old, most of them dead and buried.

With these ginger root hooks,
she would knead my body
to lift my fever.
She refused my American father the right
to take me to his hospital. "They butcher people alive
there, and then poison them to death.
Never trust modern doctors," she said.

For me she made tea from the hair of corn.
"Because corn is a woman, she can cure."

Secretly, in the fever time,
she slipped a small seashell
under my skin.
There, between my layers, the shell called *anting-anting*
lives and hurts me.
It is her gift, this pain
migrating toward my heart,
as I grow to become a crone.

At night it drives me from sleep, pushes me away
from the comfort of pillows and white sheets,
sends me to stare
at luminous lights in the black sky,
and gives me courage to write the stories of women.

There is no way to write a poem about hot flashes.

Now you know why I am forced,
to weave an imploding star pattern
into the future.

GASPING FOR AIR

Hearsay in the Holy Land,
crib of many beliefs:
Each woman who died in childbirth
was remembered by the planting
of a single cedar seed.

The fragrant forest was enormous.
Twisted, ancient trees,
left lung of the planet. Some cut
to build mighty ships or
line the temple walls of King Solomon,
bent low by the wind,
in arboreal effort to hug.

I like to imagine
that ancient peoples
inventing religions
would honor the mothers lost.

Related to the Cedars of Lebanon
are the tall, slender, Asian-American
thuja trees.
From these red and white evergreens
we have durable timber,
but no fruit at all.

Women use the sap of thuja
to make a homeopathic medicine for rape.

Cranes flying over our planet
have proclaimed, "We are running out of trees."
They prefer not to roost on phone wires.

We moderns forgot to commemorate lost mothers.
Had we remembered,
there would be no shortage of oxygen.

Anniversary Poem

The genie of this poem
was born from the exhaust of an old diesel truck
flying down the road,
between Denpasar and Jakarta.

I hugged your body tightly
as we rode behind it on a motorbike, in the rain.
We chased the truck a while,
and just as we passed it, this poem flipped
up from the mud flaps, and blew
black and smoky in my face.

I had no paper or pen
to record the genius of line and cadence.
You drove faster to keep up with it, escaping,
nails of rain beating our poncho to tatters.

I have forgotten most of the words,
but remember it was our anniversary,
nineteen years of shared song,
sorrows, children, construction, batik
and some scars we both admit to.
I would wash the tattoos of anger off of my skin,
if only the ink were not indelible.
I pray the indigo has not penetrated my bones.

When we first touched,
my skin was dolphin smooth and blue,
I was shy, unaware our youth had limits.
You, were a beautiful bright eyed man
with an ukulele.

Still, after decades, behind a silver beard,
I find you fragrant as a pheromone garden,
delicious as a tangerine.

Today I Must Resurrect My Sister's Baby

The persimmons in Great-grandfather's village
in China, would be ripening perfectly.
Her dark hair would have the orange highlights
of our shared Irish blood.

Great-grandmother, Iva Mae, would not recognize
the half-Korean beauty as her family,
yet the Filipinos on mother's side would be proud to love her.

Maybe she would spend her birthday summer
in a small town outside of Seoul,
taking care of paternal grandparents, eating the foods
of ancestors, and teaching them a few words in English.

Her brothers would have made specialties,
Asian foods, uncommonly spiced for *Mei-Mei*.
I would embroider flying birds on her pockets.

Bringing my sister home, after two decades
of trying, has never worked.
There is no vehicle, save the body,
in which a soul may travel.
In every dream
I am forced to leave her at the graveyard,
pregnant.

My sister's baby would be turning twenty this August,
had she been born, and had she lived.

We put a tiny baptismal dress in my sister's coffin.
The white lace must now be yellow,
I hid blue butterflies under the hem.
The family was crying for losing Christine,
I wanted to hold her baby.

This morning, I have finally cried,
for all the wind that never blew through her unlived days.
Of all our family languages, she only knew the syntax of dark womb.
She never knew the taste of Mother's milk,
but I am certain, she knew my sister's voice singing.

I am still holding an invisible red thread,
the other end of it is held tightly
in never-born Baby's hand.

EllyAnna's Story Cloth

Upon the birth of a girl child—
see her life threads
warped onto the loom in shades
of purple responsibilities, indigo forbiddens, pale brown sorrows.
Feel the weight of recipes calling for two cups of sugar
when she only has one.

But when she opens her eyes
for the first time,
I sense the golden weft
the over and under
of intention, invention,
and true love that she will weave
across each moment and movement of her days.

The yardage of her life's story cloth
will shimmer and change
when sunlight strikes it.

In the darkness
her colors will rest,
and keep us warm.

Won't Need to Say a Word

In 1978 I lost the honey bear.
It was sitting on the windowsill,
sunlight trying to penetrate the thicker golden,
then it was gone.
I found her in the garden.
Baby was squeezing the viscous sweet
onto the backs of big zucchinis.
Lying on her belly,
she was tasting sweet green stripes.
Inside my chest is a snapshot
of the dirt stuck to her two-year-old face
when she turned toward me that summer.

Tonight my daughter sleeps.
Blue parchment eyelids
fold over all she has seen
and kiss her vision goodnight.
I inspect her arms, finding some purple.
Curled between her breasts
my granddaughter exhales,
then her breath stutters in again.
They smell unhappy.

This is my house enfolding them.
So I sip a hot cup of vinegar,
counting my strong feelings,
watching them hanker for blood.
So many scarlet demons
hunch down
in the mud trenches of my heart.

Once, when this girl
was still eating at my breasts,
I prayed for the mother
of the man my daughter would marry.
I hoped that wherever she was,
she would love her son enough,
enough to teach him tenderness,
manners, loyalty.
She taught him to love black cars and guns.

I forgot to give my daughter a filter.
I forgot to say, "Some people are just plain bad."

Sitting in the morning garden,
before they wake,
I make a witch's plan to feed my generations:
Borage flowers, like cobalt stars to guide them;
Kale, nourishing, curly and bitter green, like life;
Fat tomatoes, circled by purple
and yellow Johnny-jump-ups.
The new baby can watch the corn
reaching toward August.

Ibu Robin Lim... was born in 1956 when a Filipino, Chinese woman married a German, Irish, Native American, against all advice.

She now lives in Indonesia where she is called; "Ibu Robin" (Mother Robin). Lim is a Certified Professional Midwife, with the North American Registry of Midwives and Ikatan Bidan Indonesia. She devotes her life to Yayasan Bumi Sehat, a not for profit organization with clinics in Bali and Aceh, www.bumisehatbali.org, www.robinlimsupport.org.

Along with receiving babies, Ibu Robin is an author of books in the childbirth genre, in both English and Bahasa Indonesia. Lim has two published chapbooks of poetry, *Stretch Marks* and *As a Child in the Religion of Gratitude*, she was a contributor to the *Tsunami Notebook* (Half Angel Press, Bali, Indonesia, 2005). Also published in 2006 by Half Angel; *Obat Asli . . . the Traditional Healing Herbs of Bali*.

In September 2009, Robin's novel, *Butterfly People*, was released by Anvil Press, in the Philippines. Ibu Robin's new book, *Placenta . . . the Forgotten Chakra*, promises to make gentle birth more gentle.

Robin's support and inspiration is her family, husband Wil, eight astounding children; Déjà, Nöel, Zhòu, Lakota, Zion, Thoreau, Hanoman, Ellyanna and two grandchildren, Zhòuie Martinez and Bodhi Padma Edzra Banjo Bernhardt, plus one more on the way.

In 2011, Lim was named a CNN Hero for her work in maternal and child health in Indonesia and disaster zones. Ibu Robin's passion is "Building Peace on Earth, One Baby, One Mother, One Family at a time."

Printed in The United States of America

CPSIA information can be obtained at www.ICGtesting.com
Printed in the USA
LVOW122056171012

303363LV00004B/2/P